A CALL TO

DISCIPLESHIP

JENNIFER B. ALLEN

Copyright© [2025] Jennifer B. Allen

Foreword

By Chancellor Winford Thompson, School of the Great Commission Bible College and Seminary

In today's world, the call to discipleship in Christ demands more than just words; it requires open hearts, unwavering compassion, and, above all, inclusivity. The Call to Discipleship by Dr. Jennifer Bruce Allen invites us to confront the tensions within the Christian community regarding inclusivity, particularly towards marginalized groups like the LGBTQ community. In doing so, she does not shy away from the complexity of the topic but addresses it with both grace and conviction.

This book thoughtfully navigates two distinct approaches that often polarize the Church. The liberal approach, which emphasizes acceptance and inclusivity, sometimes at the expense of addressing sin, and the legalistic approach, which strictly adheres to Scripture but may inadvertently exclude those whom Christ himself welcomed. Dr. Allen's dedication to fostering understanding between these perspectives is a testament to her commitment to the heart of Christ's ministry—loving one another as God loves us.

In this forward, I feel compelled to remind us that we are all, indeed, God's children. Scripture tells us there is no sin too large or too small, no person too righteous or too flawed, to be excluded from God's love. Just as God created each of us uniquely, He calls us to Him without stipulations or exclusions. The beauty of His love is that it is a love without bounds. Christ Himself proclaimed, "Whosoever will let them come," opening the door for each of us to embrace Him fully, regardless of our backgrounds, identities, or struggles.

In The *Call to Discipleship*, Dr. Allen dares to ask challenging questions: How do we genuinely include everyone in the body of Christ? How do we embody a faith that is both inclusive and transformative? These questions are essential for the Church today, and Dr. Allen's book provides a framework for us to explore them deeply, with humility and authenticity.

I commend Dr. Jennifer Bruce Allen for her courage in tackling this essential conversation and for offering us a pathway toward a discipleship that reflects the boundless love of our Savior. May her words inspire us all to live with open hearts, to welcome with open arms, and to remember that true discipleship is a call to love, include, and embrace every single one of God's children.

Foreword

As the days become more perilous, believers must be prepared to both evangelize and disciple those that battle with LGBTQ issues. Dr. Allen's work confronts, counsels and provides helpful insights to do just that. We can either retreat or reach out.

Deliverance is possible, let's work while it is day and make people find real freedom.

Bishop Anthony Pelt

Senior Pastor Radiant Living Worship Center

Prelude:

The Mandate of Discipleship

Discipleship is not optional; it is a mandate given to us by Jesus Christ. Every believer is called to it. We all need discipleship it is the process of growth, teaching, and refinement that shapes us into the perfected vessels Christ will return for. Discipleship keeps us near the cross, fixes our eyes on God, and is vital for our spiritual survival, especially in these uncertain times. Now, more than ever, the church must embrace discipleship.

Many criticize the church for focusing on preaching within its four walls, saying, "Y'all are just preaching to the choir." But the truth is, the choir needs it too. Discipleship is for the saints. While evangelism reaches the lost, discipleship strengthens and equips the body of Christ. We must return to the heart of discipleship because people are hurting, confused, and afraid. The world is facing unprecedented challenges, and now is the time for the church to rise not just in teaching, but in investing in others and guiding them through transformation.

While discipleship is for everyone, I carry a deep burden for those struggling with homosexuality and identity confusion. I know firsthand that this is a spiritual battle a deceptive stronghold that blinds individuals, trapping them in an internal war for their very souls. This book was birthed from that burden, recognizing that the harvest is plentiful and that people are coming into the church with real struggles, real wounds, and real strongholds. They need more than just sermons they need intercessors, mentors, and spiritual warriors who will stand in the gap, pray them through, and walk with them as God brings transformation.

Not everyone in the LGBTQ community is content with their lifestyle. Some are searching for true fulfillment but have yet to find it. Others wrestle deeply with identity confusion and long for clarity. They need people who can see beyond the surface, discerning the spiritual battles at play and calling out strongholds in the power of Jesus' name. Deliverance is possible, but it requires patience, wisdom, and a church willing to disciple with both truth and love.

This book is my gift to the church. It has been two years in the making, and the spiritual attacks I endured while writing it were relentless. Yet, I know this is the season for its release appointed for such a time as this. The church must be prepared to disciple those who are seeking freedom, and that preparation begins with understanding the true call of discipleship. The harvest is coming, and it is time to equip the body of Christ to receive it.

Introduction

One of the most contentious issues facing the Body of Christ today is its approach to discipling individuals within the LGBTQ community particularly those who earnestly desire to serve God yet wrestle with same-sex attraction. These individuals often experience deep inner conflict as they struggle to reconcile their identity with their sincere longing to please God.

This tension is not only deeply personal but has also become a point of public debate. In recent years, concerns surrounding this community have ignited national conversations and reached the highest levels of governance, including the United States Supreme Court. Legal battles over equality, marriage rights, and anti-discrimination laws have placed the Christian faith under global scrutiny, often positioning churches in difficult and divisive situations. With the current presidential administration, these debates have intensified even further.

The challenge we face as followers of Christ is this: How do we remain faithful to the teachings of the Bible while extending compassion and grace to those in the LGBTQ community who seek to know God? At the end of it all, our allegiance is not to any political party or its ideologies we take our instructions from God.

As believers, we are called to make disciples of all people—without exception. Jesus' command in Matthew 28:19-20 is clear: we are to go into all the world, making disciples of all nations, baptizing them, and teaching them to obey God's commandments. Yet, in practice, many churches have struggled to fully embrace this calling when it comes to the LGBTQ community. Too often, a lack of understanding leads to responses that fall into two extremes either harsh rejection that pushes people away or excessive leniency that blurs the lines of biblical truth.

This issue is further complicated by the cultural shifts unfolding today. What was once considered morally unacceptable is now widely celebrated across many sectors of society. The LGBTQ community has gained increasing support from influential allies in media, politics, and even some religious circles. As a result, many within the Body of Christ find themselves uncertain about how to respond caught between societal pressure to embrace these new norms and the biblical call to uphold God's design for human relationships and sexuality.

The church today faces a pressing question: What is the most effective and Christ-centered way to disciple members of the LGBTQ community? How can we uphold biblical standards of righteousness while extending the same love, grace, and hope that Jesus offered to every sinner—without discrimination?

Jeffrey R. Scott, in his research, identifies three primary approaches to addressing this issue. The first is the liberal approach, which prioritizes acceptance and inclusivity, often at the expense of addressing sin and the need for repentance. The second is the legalistic approach, which strictly adheres to Scripture but can sometimes lack compassion, driving people away with its rigidity. The third and the approach I believe holds the most promise—is a balanced one: upholding the truth of Scripture while recognizing the inherent dignity of those we seek to disciple.

In the chapters ahead, I will examine each of these approaches in depth, drawing from my personal experiences, biblical study, and research. My aim is to provide a thoughtful, biblically sound perspective on how the church can better serve this community while remaining faithful to the teachings of Christ. This is not merely a theoretical discussion—it has real-life implications for those within the church and the broader community. My prayer is that through this exploration, the Body of Christ will be equipped to share the transformative power of Jesus with those who need Him most, all while remaining steadfast in the truth of His Word.

Table of Contents

Chapter 1: The Liberal Approach

The liberal approach to discipling members of the LGBTQ community within the church prioritizes inclusivity and acceptance, striving to create a welcoming environment where everyone feels embraced, regardless of their lifestyle or struggles. Often referred to as the "acceptance" approach, this method intentionally minimizes or disregards the biblical view of homosexuality, emphasizing instead God's unconditional love for all people.

At first glance, this approach may seem compassionate and Christ-like. After all, Jesus spent much of His ministry with those society considered outcasts tax collectors, prostitutes, and sinners of every kind. He never shamed them or made them feel unwelcome. Instead, He drew them near, offering love, hope, and the opportunity for transformation. In a similar way, the liberal approach seeks to extend that same love and friendship to the LGBTQ community, ensuring they feel included within the Body of Christ.

However, while this method highlights love and belonging, it often neglects essential aspects of discipleship, such as repentance, sanctification, and obedience to God's Word.

By focusing primarily on acceptance, it can avoid difficult but necessary conversations about spiritual growth and transformation both of which are foundational to a life of faith.

Scripture demonstrates that Jesus' love was never separate from His call to repentance. In John 8, when He showed mercy to the woman caught in adultery, He refused to condemn her but also gave a clear command: "Go now and leave your life of sin" (John 8:11). This delicate balance between grace and truth is essential in discipleship. While it is vital to love individuals in the midst of their struggles, we are also called to guide them toward a deeper relationship with God a relationship that requires surrender, repentance, and change.

Over time, the liberal approach has led to significant shifts within some denominations. Many churches have fully embraced and affirmed the LGBTQ community without calling for transformation. For example, in 2013, the Christian Church (Disciples of Christ) voted to welcome practicing LGBTQ individuals into all areas of church life, including leadership, and affirmed same-sex marriages. Similarly, the Episcopal Church took steps toward inclusion, beginning in 2009 by developing resources for same-sex blessings. By 2012, they officially began blessing same-sex marriages, and by 2015, they removed the traditional definition of marriage as a union between one man and one woman.

While some view this approach as progressive and inclusive, it raises serious theological concerns. In its eagerness to embrace everyone, it deviates from core Christian beliefs as laid out in the Bible. It often prioritizes social and political ideologies over the sacred, covenantal relationship that discipleship is meant to foster. By being overly permissive with sin including homosexuality the church risks causing more harm than good. It fails to teach that sin, in any form, breaks the holy covenant between an individual and God.

Scripture reminds us of this truth in Isaiah 59:2: "But your iniquities have separated you from your God; your sins have hidden His face from you so that He will not hear." While nothing can separate us from God's love, sin still creates a divide between us and Him. Ignoring this truth, especially in the context of discipleship, does a disservice to those who genuinely seek a deeper relationship with God. True discipleship must not only welcome people as they are but also guide them toward who God has called them to be.

The Bible is clear in its teachings on homosexuality, identifying it as sin. As disciples of Christ, we have a responsibility to stand firm on biblical truths. In its attempt to be welcoming, the liberal approach often blurs these truths, preventing people from understanding the weight of sin and the need for transformation.

I have personally observed a rise in same-sex marriages within Christian leadership roles, particularly in churches that have embraced this overly accepting stance. The liberal approach, coupled with increasing divisions within the Body of Christ, makes it challenging to speak out against these trends without being labeled hateful or homophobic. Yet, as believers, we are called to uphold God's truth with grace and love.

This ideology closely aligns with one of the seven churches in the book of Revelation: the church of Thyatira, as described in Revelation 2:18-29. This church was commended for its love, service, patience, and endurance. However, despite these virtues, God rebuked them for tolerating Jezebel, a woman who called herself a prophetess and led believers into sexual immorality and idolatry.

As you are aware, when we speak of Jezebel here, we are referring to the spirit of Jezebel, not the individual. Although this spirit is not a marine spirit, it is heavily influenced by one, particularly Leviathan, who is described as the father of the children of pride. Marine spirits often bring sexual sin and immorality, fostering the lust of the eyes, the lust of the flesh, and the pride of life. The church in Thyatira was rebuked for allowing this Jezebel spirit to take root in their community, tolerating blatant sin and false teaching.

In a similar way, churches today under a liberal ideology risk falling into the same error. They present a false teaching by failing to share the full truth of God's Word. Like the church in Thyatira, these liberal churches are in danger of compromising holiness, which deeply grieves the Lord. Just as the church of Thyatira was called to repent in Revelation, so too is God calling these churches today to repentance.

Failing to do so distorts God's truth, providing a false sense of security rather than genuine transformation through His Word.

This challenge naturally leads us to consider the next approach in the conversation on discipleship: the legalistic approach.

Chapter 2: The Legalistic Approach

The legalistic approach to dealing with homosexuality within the church takes a firm stance, using the Bible as its primary authority. This perspective is often seen as a "rejection" approach, where the main goal is to uphold God's moral standards at all costs. As Jeffrey R. Scott pointed out, "This approach rests heavily on the belief that the church's responsibility is to protect God's moral standards at all costs." While rooted in a desire to remain faithful to Scripture, this method often comes across as harsh, sometimes even homophobic, focusing more on condemnation than compassion.

I have witnessed this legalistic attitude firsthand, where certain sins especially visible ones like homosexuality—are elevated above others. Some church communities have treated homosexuality as the ultimate sin, often citing scriptures like Leviticus 18:22, which calls it an "abomination" or "detestable" in various translations. Passages like these, along with the story of Sodom and Gomorrah, where God destroys cities due to rampant sin (including homosexual activity), have fueled a rigid and sometimes hostile stance toward the LGBTQ community. Genesis 19:3-5 describes how the men of Sodom lusted after angels sent by God, leading to further interpretations that equate homosexuality with divine judgment:

"Before they had gone to bed, all the men from every part of the city of Sodom both young and old surrounded the house. They called to Lot, 'Where are the men who came to you tonight? Bring them out to us so that we can have sex with them.'" (Genesis 19:4-5, NIV)

It is easy to see how passages like this can stoke fear and intolerance, leading many churches to use these scriptures to justify rejection and judgment. But is this truly the right approach?

While it is true that we are called to preach the unadulterated Word of God, we are also commanded to do so with love. Jesus, in Matthew 11:28, extends an open invitation to all: "Come to me, all you who are weary and burdened, and I will give you rest." Nowhere in this invitation does He exclude anyone, including those struggling with homosexuality. To reject anyone who is genuinely seeking God's truth goes against the very spirit of Christ's message.

The legalistic approach often confuses the role of the church in an individual's transformation. We are not called to change people ourselves—that is God's work. As Paul wrote in 1 Corinthians 3:6-7, "I planted the seed, Apollos watered it, but God has been making it grow." The believer's job is to plant or water the seed of the Gospel, not to force spiritual growth or transformation. Only God has the power to change hearts, and it is essential to remember this when discipling anyone, regardless of their struggles.

Rejecting or condemning someone before they even have a chance to encounter God's grace is not biblical. The church is meant to be a place of healing, not exclusion. Suggesting that someone must first be "free from sin" before they can be welcomed into the church contradicts the very essence of the Gospel, which is about inviting broken people to the Healer.

Of course, the Bible also speaks to the importance of church discipline. In 1 Corinthians 5:11-13, Paul instructs the church to distance itself from those who persist in sin:

"But now I am writing to you that you must not associate with anyone who claims to be a brother or sister but is sexually immoral or greedy, an idolater or slanderer, a drunkard or swindler. Do not even eat with such people. What business is it of mine to judge those outside the church? Are you not to judge those inside? God will judge those outside. 'Expel the wicked person from among you.'"

At first glance, this might seem to justify the harsh stance of the legalistic approach. However, Paul was addressing persistent, unrepentant sin within the church, not those seeking repentance and transformation. This distinction is critical. A repentant heart longs for God's grace, while a rebellious spirit refuses to submit to God's authority. The church must be careful not to confuse the two.

As Alan Shlemon points out, Jesus provided a clear framework for addressing sin within the church in Matthew 18:15-17:

1. Confront the sinner in private. If they acknowledge their sin and repent, rejoice.

2. If they don't listen, bring another believer or two. Call out the sin again with witnesses.

3. If they still refuse to repent, bring the matter before the church.

4. If they continue in rebellion, dismiss them from the church— treat them as a gentile or tax collector.

The goal is always restoration, not rejection. Ideally, the process ends at step one with private repentance and reconciliation. However, a legalistic approach often rushes to step four, causing unnecessary division and harm.

While legalism may stem from a sincere desire to uphold God's standards, it risks overlooking the bigger picture: God's heart for restoration. Sin must be addressed, but always with grace, patience, and a genuine longing to bring people into a right relationship with God. When we lean toward judgment without love, we risk driving people further from the very transformation we seek to inspire.

Chapter 3: Hypocrisy in the Church

One of the most troubling issues I've observed in the church is the presence of selective discipline a double standard that exposes the hypocrisy embedded in many church communities. Churches often impose harsher discipline on certain sins or individuals while turning a blind eye to others. This selective approach not only contradicts the principles of justice and fairness but also damages the church's credibility as a place of healing and transformation.

A glaring example of this hypocrisy is the way churches treat young women who become pregnant outside of marriage. In many congregations, especially in traditional settings, these women are brought before the church to be publicly shamed. They are expected to confess their "sin" before the entire congregation, as if their transgression warrants such extreme exposure. Meanwhile, the young man who fathered the child often a member of the same congregation is not subjected to the same treatment. More often than not, he escapes public scrutiny entirely. This disparity in how men and women are disciplined reveals a deep-rooted hypocrisy in the church's handling of sin based on gender.

This inconsistency extends far beyond issues of pregnancy. In many churches, particularly within the Black church, gay musicians, choir directors, and singers are allowed to serve in prominent roles without facing the same scrutiny as others who struggle with different sins. Despite the church's official stance on homosexuality, these individuals continue to lead worship and participate in church activities without challenge. Yet, when other sins are exposed especially those of a sexual nature the church can be quick to deliver heavy-handed judgment.

Even more troubling is the way some churches have protected prominent leaders accused of sexual misconduct, often involving young men. Rather than addressing these allegations with transparency and accountability, many churches choose to shield these leaders, allowing them to continue in ministry. In some cases, the accusers are vilified while the accused are protected, creating an environment where truth and justice are sacrificed to maintain the status quo.

A high-profile example of this is a gospel music icon whose name is synonymous with Black gospel music. This artist appeared in a film called Dirty Laundry, which was popular at Black gay pride festivals. In 2007, he publicly stated that he believed homosexuality was not a sin but a result of genetics. Despite these views, which contradicted the church's teachings, he continued to be celebrated in the gospel music industry and was even named the "Ambassador of Gospel Music." This selective acceptance of certain individuals, despite their open rejection of church doctrine, further exposes the deep-rooted hypocrisy within the church.

There are other prominent figures within the church who have been speculated to struggle with same-sex attraction, and many of these leaders have been accused of sexual assault against young men and women within their congregations and choirs. Despite these serious allegations, some have continued their ministries without ever being held accountable. This is yet another example of the church failing to address sin consistently and transparently, choosing instead to protect its own while neglecting the need for justice and healing.

The legalistic approach within the church is further undermined by hypocrisy. Discipline is often applied selectively, targeting certain sins while overlooking others based on an individual's rank or title. This creates a culture of inconsistency and favoritism, which directly contradicts the fairness and justice that God commands.

The truth is that all sin is significant in God's eyes. The church cannot afford to treat some sins with an iron rod while ignoring others, nor should discipline be applied only to those without status while excusing prominent figures. If the church is to reflect God's character, it must embody His fairness and justice. As James 2:1 reminds us, "My brothers and sisters, believers in our glorious Lord Jesus Christ must not show favoritism."

Church discipline should never be about shaming or excluding individuals; rather, it should be rooted in a desire for restoration. Discipline must always aim to lead people back to Christ, not push them further away. Too often, the church's approach is punitive rather than redemptive, leaving individuals more wounded than they were before. This is not the heart of God.

As believers, we are called to hold each other accountable, but we must do so with love, grace, and fairness. Hypocrisy within the church undermines this calling and damages its witness to the world. Without consistency and fairness, double standards emerge, weakening the church's credibility. Addressing this issue is crucial, as God is a God of justice, and we are called to be a people of fairness in all things.

Before moving on to the next chapter, it is important to address the issue of hypocrisy in the church. In the following discussion, we will explore another prevalent approach that is becoming increasingly common within the body of Christ. While it may seem neutral and unbiased, it still falls outside the will of God. This is what I refer to as the "silent approach."

Chapter 4: The Silent Approach

There's another approach I've witnessed within the church that must be addressed: the silent approach. This approach involves believers who choose not to take a position on the issue of homosexuality, or any sin for that matter. They remain silent on both sides, neither condemning nor affirming, seemingly attempting to avoid conflict or controversy. At first glance, this may seem like a neutral stance, a way to "keep the peace," but in reality, it is a dangerous form of disengagement. It fails the very essence of discipleship.

True discipleship demands a commitment to both truth and transformation. As the Body of Christ, when we fail to confront sin, we abandon those in need of guidance, leaving them lost and directionless. The silent approach may appear compassionate, disguising itself as respect for personal boundaries, but in reality, it withholds the very lifeline that could lead someone to freedom and a deeper relationship with God.

The common refrain often goes, "I don't have a problem with homosexuals." While it's true that we should never take issue with the person who is struggling, it is equally true that we must address the sin that holds them captive. As disciples, our role is not to judge or condemn but to serve as instruments of God's grace, extending a path to freedom from spiritual bondage. Sin, in any form, separates individuals from God. When we remain silent, we ignore the spiritual danger they face, effectively leaving them trapped without hope of deliverance.

Isaiah 59:2 states clearly: "But your iniquities have separated you from your God; your sins have hidden His face from you so that He will not hear." Sin whether sexual immorality, pride, greed, or any other form prevents people from experiencing the fullness of God's love and favor. God's detestation of sin is not selective; He does not tolerate one sin more than another. As His disciples, we must also reject whatever keeps people from Him.

Yet, the silent approach dismisses the reality of sin altogether. It is a refusal to speak truth into people's lives the very truth that can set them free. While silence may seem like the easiest way to avoid discomfort, it is not a neutral stance. In reality, it is complicity. We may convince ourselves that we are keeping the peace, but in truth, we are standing on the sidelines as people drift further into spiritual danger. By remaining silent, we deny them the opportunity for repentance and transformation.

Scripture commands us to be bold in speaking the truth. Isaiah 58:1 declares: "Cry aloud, spare not; lift up your voice like a trumpet; tell My people their transgression, and the house of Jacob their sins." Staying silent is the very opposite of what God has called us to do.

Confronting sin may be uncomfortable, but love compels us to act. In this case, silence is not an act of love—it is abandonment.

In a world overflowing with voices presenting alternative truths, the church's silence leaves a void that others are eager to fill. More often than not, these voices promote ideologies that contradict the Word of God, drawing people deeper into spiritual confusion and bondage. When the church fails to speak, it allows secular philosophies ones that prioritize human desires over divine commandments to dominate, drowning out the truth of God's Word.

One of the greatest dangers of remaining silent is that it often stems from a fear of man rather than a fear of God. In today's culture, topics like homosexuality are incredibly sensitive, and the pressure to conform to societal norms can feel overwhelming. Many believers remain silent, fearing they will be labeled judgmental, homophobic, or intolerant. However, as disciples of Christ, our ultimate priority must be to honor God rather than seek approval from people. Proverbs 29:25 reminds us: "The fear of man lays a snare, but whoever trusts in the Lord is safe."

We must not let the fear of offending others prevent us from speaking the truth in love. Jesus Himself never hesitated to share hard truths, even when they led to discomfort or division. His love was inseparable from His call to repentance. When He spoke to the adulterous woman, He said, "Go now and leave your life of sin" (John 8:11). He did not condemn her, but neither did He ignore her sin. Instead, He offered her a path to redemption.

When we remain silent, we withhold the very opportunity for deliverance. Silence can imply indifference or worse, approval. It allows sin to go unchallenged. As disciples, our mission is not to condemn, but neither is it to turn a blind eye. Ephesians 4:15 reminds us to "speak the truth in love." This is the heart of effective discipleship: a balance of grace and truth. Without both, we fall short of our calling.

The silent approach not only implies indifference but also suggests that the truth is not worth defending. Yet, Jesus declares in Matthew 10:32-33, "Whoever acknowledges me before others, I will also acknowledge before my Father in heaven. But whoever disowns me before others, I will disown before my Father in heaven." In moments of moral and spiritual crisis, our silence may amount to disowning the truth both of who God is and of what He has commanded us to uphold.

Finally, we must recognize that silence comes at an eternal cost. When we withhold the truth, we deny others the chance to experience the fullness of God's grace. We deprive them of the opportunity to be transformed by His love. The stakes could not be higher. As Paul writes in Romans 10:14, "How, then, can they call on the one they have not believed in? And how can they believe in the one of whom they have not heard? And how can they hear without someone preaching to them?"

Remaining silent is not an option for disciples who are committed to their mission. We cannot afford to stand on the sidelines. We must rise above our fears, discomfort, and cultural pressures to fully engage with the truth of the gospel. It is our love for people and, more importantly, our love for God that compels us to speak.

In conclusion, while silence may seem like a way to avoid conflict, it ultimately causes greater harm. It allows sin to flourish unchecked, prevents spiritual growth, and reflects a failure to live out our calling as disciples of Christ. We are called to engage the world with both the truth and the love of Christ, offering people not just acceptance, but transformation. The cost of silence is too great both for us and for those we are called to reach.

Chapter 5: The Balanced Approach

The balanced approach to discipleship, as Jeffrey Scott explains, strives to uphold God's moral standards while also embracing people where they are, guiding them toward spiritual transformation. He notes, "This approach acknowledges that life-dominating sins rarely disappear overnight, even after genuine biblical repentance. Instead, freedom unfolds through a process."

This perspective emphasizes that transformation is a journey rather than an instant change and underscores the importance of patience, grace, and truth working together in every believer's life

A balanced approach is essential to true discipleship. The church must find a harmonious middle ground between grace and judgment. An overemphasis on grace, without a call to repentance or accountability, may lead individuals astray, fostering a false sense of security in their sin. Conversely, excessive judgment, devoid of love and understanding, can alienate people from the church, leaving them feeling condemned and abandoned.

When discipling new converts, regardless of their struggles whether same-sex attraction or any other sin balance is crucial. We are called to "rightly divide the word of truth" (2 Timothy 2:15), but we must do so with God's love and grace at the forefront. Jesus exemplified this balance in His ministry, demonstrating how to embrace people while simultaneously calling them to a higher standard of holiness.

One of the clearest expressions of how we are to disciple with love is found in 1 Corinthians 13:4-5, which states:

"Love is patient, love is kind. It does not envy, it does not boast, it is not proud. It does not dishonor others, it is not self-seeking, it is not easily angered, it keeps no record of wrongs." (NIV)

Love is at the heart of true discipleship. Yet, too often, fear and misunderstanding corrupt this love. Within the church, homophobia like racism and other forms of prejudice can distort the truth of God's Word. The reality is that love and hate cannot coexist; one will always drive out the other. If we are to obey Christ's command to love one another, we must confront and remove fear and prejudice from our hearts. As 1 John 4:18 reminds us, "There is no fear in love. But perfect love drives out fear."

A balanced approach to discipleship requires that we carry each other's burdens, as instructed in Galatians 6:2. Every struggle whether rooted in sin or personal hardship becomes a shared burden among brothers and sisters in Christ. When viewed this way, discipleship transforms into a journey of mutual support and encouragement. We are called to sharpen one another, just as iron sharpens iron (Proverbs 27:17), helping each other grow into the fullness of Christ. This means addressing sin not with judgment, but with compassion not to condemn, but to restore.

One of the greatest dangers in discipleship is the tendency to judge others harshly based on our personal standards or experiences. Pulaski and Lihn caution us:

"Do not judge others by your own standards, perspective, or experiences, for you will be judged in the same manner in which you judge them. Instead, form a just judgment by first examining your own spirit. Only then can you position yourself to help restore those who may be at fault, if necessary." (Matthew 7:1-2) This wisdom is essential for approaching discipleship with humility and grace. We must always remember that we, too, have received undeserved grace from God, and it is our responsibility to extend that same grace to others.

Compassion is the foundation of a balanced approach. Genuine compassion begins by reflecting on our own experiences with God's mercy. How can we judge others harshly when we ourselves have been met with such kindness and patience from God? Balance does not mean overlooking sin but rather addressing it with the same love, wisdom, and grace that God has shown us.

Wisdom also plays a vital role in this approach. We need discernment to separate the sin from the soul. Homosexuality, like any other sin, is often treated as if it were a sickness or disease, but at its core, it is a form of spiritual bondage. As Ephesians 6:12 reminds us:

"For our struggle is not against flesh and blood, but against the rulers, against the authorities, against the powers of this dark world, and against the spiritual forces of evil in the heavenly realms."

The ultimate goal should be deliverance and freedom not condemnation or shame.

Deliverance comes when we recognize that our battle is not against individuals but against the spiritual strongholds that bind them. A balanced approach keeps this in mind, offering love and support to the person while actively working against the sin that entangles them. This perspective acknowledges that transformation is a process one that requires time, patience, and the steady application of both grace and truth.

In conclusion, the balanced approach to discipleship follows the biblical model of Christ. It calls for both grace and truth, love and accountability. It seeks not to condemn but to restore. It recognizes that spiritual growth is a journey, not an instant change. As disciples of Christ, we must be patient, compassionate, and wise in leading others on this path always keeping in mind the ultimate goal: helping them find freedom and deliverance in Christ.

Chapter 6: You Can't Counsel Demons, *Deliverance is Needed*

The content of this book is rooted in the testimonies of individuals who once engaged in same-sex immorality but have since experienced deliverance. These powerful stories highlight a critical issue the church's failure to effectively disciple those in the LGBTQ community who are struggling with profound spiritual battles. For too long, the church has leaned on counseling, discussions, and passive approaches, when what is truly needed is spiritual deliverance.

Many in the LGBTQ community are crying out for help some audibly, others in silence as they wrestle with homosexuality, a struggle that often conceals a deeper spiritual conflict. These individuals are not merely seeking identity or societal acceptance; they are engaged in a battle against unseen forces. Their lives can become vulnerable to spiritual influences, exposing them to mental, emotional, and even physical attacks. This is why counseling alone falls short when spiritual bondage is present, only deliverance can bring lasting freedom.

The consequences of these spiritual battles manifest in various destructive ways, including substance abuse, mental health struggles, and even acts of violence. Research conducted by the Centers for Disease Control and Prevention (CDC) reveals an alarming reality lesbian, gay, and bisexual youth are more than twice as likely to attempt suicide compared to their heterosexual peers. A range of factors, including exposure to hostile environments, contribute to the mental and emotional distress they experience.

The statistics surrounding sexual violence are staggering. Approximately 40% of gay men and 47% of bisexual men have experienced sexual violence (excluding rape) at some point in their lives. Additionally, studies indicate that 26% of gay men and 37% of bisexual men have endured intimate partner violence. These alarming numbers underscore the deep trauma many within the LGBTQ community are facing. Whether they realize it or not, many are searching for answers seeking freedom from the darkness that grips their lives.

The church must recognize that this issue extends far beyond social or psychological concerns. The battles waged within the LGBTQ community are profoundly spiritual, and spiritual struggles require spiritual solutions. Deliverance is not merely a hopeful suggestion it is a biblical mandate for breaking the chains of spiritual bondage. As Ephesians 6:12 reminds us:

"For our struggle is not against flesh and blood, but against the rulers, against the authorities, against the powers of this dark world and against the spiritual forces of evil in the heavenly realms."

The church can no longer afford to view these individuals solely as "abominations" or as beyond redemption. Instead, we must see them as souls in need of deliverance souls that God deeply loves and longs to redeem. Jesus did not come to save the righteous; He came to seek and save the lost. It is time for the church to reclaim its role in setting the captives free through the power of the Holy Spirit.

It is crucial to make a distinction here: standing firm on God's Word does not equate to endorsing sin, nor does it mean becoming a sympathizer of the LGBTQ movement. Rather, it means extending compassion to those ensnared in spiritual bondage, recognizing that they are not the enemy the sin and spiritual forces at work behind it are. As disciples, our mission is to lead the lost to the saving power of Christ, and that begins by seeing the person, not just the sin.

The testimonies of those who have experienced deliverance from same-sex attraction serve as a powerful reminder of God's transformative power when the church rises in love and truth. Many of these individuals have publicly shared their stories, bearing witness to the reality that God not only can but does bring people out of spiritual darkness. Once bound by their desires, they found true freedom through the power of the Holy Spirit.

One truth remains undeniable: deliverance is essential. While counseling has its place and compassion is necessary, neither can replace the power of the Holy Spirit to break chains and restore lives.

The church must reclaim its foundation in deliverance ministry, recognizing that this battle is ultimately spiritual and must be fought with spiritual weapons. As 2 Corinthians 10:4 declares, "The weapons we fight with are not the weapons of the world. On the contrary, they have divine power to demolish strongholds."

The journey to freedom for those in the LGBTQ community is not an easy one. It demands patience, love, and the undeniable power of God to bring lasting transformation. The church must be willing to engage in this battle with the full conviction that deliverance is not merely an option it is a necessity. Only through the supernatural work of deliverance can individuals break free from spiritual oppression and step into the abundant life that God has designed for them.

Testimonies

These testimonies are available on YouTube and are also referenced in the appendix of this book. The purpose of sharing these stories is not to harm anyone but to proclaim the transformative power of God. For this reason, only the first names of the testifiers will be included. If you would like more information about each individual, feel free to use the links in the appendix to hear more of their story.

First Testimony: Luis

Luis shares that he has always struggled with same-sex attraction. As a child, he was often bullied and rejected for being seen as different he preferred playing with girls rather than boys.

Luis explains that his parents became Christians and started attending church. During this time, while still grappling with his same-sex attraction, he learned that homosexuality was condemned, leaving him conflicted. Despite understanding the consequences of what he had been taught was sin, he found himself pulled deeper into that lifestyle, which led to turmoil. His circumstances worsened until he became homeless, eventually turning to prostitution to survive.

One night, while wandering the streets, Luis stumbled into a church. A woman prayed for him, and in that moment, he surrendered his life to God. However, the next morning, he felt disheartened when he woke up still attracted to men he had expected his desires to vanish overnight.

Later, Luis was invited to Pulse nightclub in Orlando, Florida—the night of the tragic mass shooting that claimed 49 lives. Miraculously, he escaped unharmed and believes that God protected him that night.

Deeply shaken by the incident, Luis turned to God, praying earnestly for change. In response, he felt God urging him to stop fixating on his sexuality and instead focus on building a relationship with Him. As

Luis shifted his attention to loving God, he noticed a profound transformation taking place.

Today, he lives in freedom through Christ, sharing the gospel with others in the LGBTQ community and helping them develop a personal relationship with Jesus.

Second Testimony: Jackie

Jackie shares that, early in life, she developed the perception that men were inconsistent and loved with conditions an idea rooted in her relationship with her father. The first affection she ever received from a man came through abuse. As a result, she grew to believe that women, by contrast, were nurturers loving, safe, and dependable. By the age of five, she began experiencing feelings of attraction toward other girls.

Jackie didn't fully understand these feelings until she attended church and heard preachers condemn homosexuality. She explains that her issue wasn't with the condemnation itself but with the harsh, mob-like way it was communicated. In response, she became rebellious in high school, embracing a homosexual lifestyle. She presented herself as a "stud," dressing and acting like a man.

At 19, despite enjoying her lifestyle, Jackie felt God calling her back to Him. Though she had no desire to become straight and wasn't interested in men, God simply told her to come and love Him. She admits that when she shifted her focus from her sexuality to her relationship with God, He began to remove the veils from her eyes (2 Corinthians 3:16).

Jackie explains that while Scripture condemned her lifestyle, it also offered hope. Today, she is married to a man and has children. Through her relationship with God, she has come to understand true conversion. Now, she shares her testimony on international platforms, helping others who struggle with same-sex attraction.

Third Testimony: Ricardo

Ricardo recalls struggling with gender identity as early as age four, being drawn to activities typically associated with girls rather than boys. By the time he reached kindergarten, he began developing feelings for other boys. Raised in a religious but not truly Christian family in Kingston, Jamaica, Ricardo grew up in a homophobic culture that left him feeling isolated and condemned.

Throughout his school life, Ricardo was bullied and often felt like giving up. By high school, boys began showing interest in him, telling him he looked like a girl. These comments planted seeds of confusion and perversion early in his life. At age 15, Ricardo was molested multiple times by a family friend, but he never told his parents out of fear they would discover he was gay.

Eventually, Ricardo embraced the LGBTQ lifestyle, feeling trapped in a world where he faced constant abuse. He began hormone therapy and breast augmentation as part of his transition to becoming a woman. However, despite these physical changes, he remained unfulfilled. Ricardo explains that he was still searching for something to fill the void until he finally heard God calling him. When he surrendered his life to Christ, God began a new work in him. Today, Ricardo testifies that through the process of transformation by the Spirit of God, his life has been renewed.

Fourth Testimony: Bosede

Bosede, a Nigerian woman, recalls that from a young age, she developed crushes on her female teachers and later on other girls. Coming from a religious family, she knew these feelings conflicted with her Christian beliefs, so she fought hard to suppress them.

In college, she decided to marry, hoping it would help her overcome her same-sex desires. She remained married for ten and a half years and had two children, but she was never truly happy. Bosede believed that if her husband had been a man of deep faith, she might have found deliverance from her struggles. After ending her marriage, she embraced a lesbian lifestyle. Her father disowned her, though her mother continued to pray for her.

As Bosede dated multiple women, searching for something to fill the void inside her, her life spiraled into chaos. She became depressed and desperate for answers. One day, she felt God speaking to her, promising that if she surrendered her life to Him, He would make her new. Overcome with emotion, she fell to her knees in her living room and pleaded for His help, asking for the strength to leave the toxic relationship she was in. She promised to serve Him for the rest of her life.

After surrendering to God, Bosede left her former church and joined one that took a balanced approach to sin. Over four years, through prayer and God's grace, she experienced deliverance from the strongholds of homosexuality.

Final Testimony: Dr. Jennifer B. Allen

In the process of discipling those who struggle with same-sex attraction or any form of identity confusion, it is crucial to recognize that these battles are deeply spiritual. My own testimony stands as a testament to the reality of this struggle.

For many years, I lived in a state of confusion and emotional pain, grappling with an identity crisis that had taken root in my heart. Throughout my life, I endured deep wounds from relationships— wounds that shaped how I viewed myself and others, especially men. I carried a great deal of hurt, anger, and mistrust, approaching relationships from a place of brokenness. Each time I entered a new relationship, I found myself trapped in the same cycle of pain, which only deepened my bitterness and left me feeling lost.

As time went on, the bitterness and pain I harbored further distorted my sense of identity. The enemy, aware of my vulnerabilities, used these emotions against me, leading me deeper into confusion. At one point, I even began to question my identity, wondering if I was attracted to women. The enemy preys on our pain, offering counterfeit solutions to our deepest wounds.

During this time, the enemy brought someone into my life—a woman who expressed interest in me. I was conflicted, feeling as though I was on the verge of stepping onto a path that was unfamiliar and contrary to everything I had been taught. Yet something held me back— something beyond my own will. I now realize it was the prayers of my grandmother, a devout woman of God, that kept me from crossing a line that would have further entangled me in confusion.

In my state of inner turmoil, I turned to my grandmother, unsure of how to move forward. I expected her to respond with condemnation or judgment, but instead, she did something that has remained with me to this day: she wept. Filled with the Holy Spirit and grounded in faith, she sat with me at her kitchen table and began to cry. She did not lecture me or chastise me. Instead, she simply cried out to God, interceding for my soul. Her compassion and prayers broke something within me.

James 5:19-20 says, "My brothers and sisters, if one of you should wander from the truth and someone should bring that person back, remember this: Whoever turns a sinner from the error of their way will save them from death and cover over a multitude of sins." My grandmother understood the power of prayer and weeping for those who were lost. Her tears were her way of fighting for me in the spiritual battle I was facing.

As she prayed, the confusion and lies the enemy had planted in my heart began to lose their grip. Her prayers, along with those of her friend who joined us, became a shield around me, protecting me from the path I had been heading toward. That day, I made the decision to walk away from the temptation before me. Though the journey was not easy and I faced many challenges afterward, I knew that God had delivered me from a spirit of confusion.

The Bible tells us in Ephesians 6:12, "For our struggle is not against flesh and blood, but against the rulers, against the authorities, against the powers of this dark world and against the spiritual forces of evil in the heavenly realms." The battle I was fighting was not merely emotional or psychological—it was deeply spiritual. The spirits of confusion, lust, and perversion are real, and they are among the most difficult to break. Yet, through the prayers of a devout, Holy Ghost-filled woman, those chains were shattered in my life.

I know firsthand how powerful these spiritual battles can be, but I also know that deliverance is possible. It wasn't condemnation that saved me it was love, prayer, and the intervention of the Holy Spirit. The enemy had sought to entangle me, but through intercession and weeping, I was set free.

As the Church, we must recognize that the struggles people face—particularly in matters of identity and attraction—are often deeply rooted in spiritual battles. These issues cannot be addressed with legalism or judgment. Instead, like my grandmother, we must weep for those who are lost and intercede for them in prayer. We must be willing to engage in spiritual warfare on their behalf, trusting that God has the power to break every chain.

The spirits of Leviathan, Python, and marine forces that operate through lust and confusion are strong, but they are no match for the power of God. Romans 8:37 reminds us, "In all these things we are more than conquerors through Him who loved us." My life is living proof that God's Spirit can deliver anyone from confusion, lust, and the lies of the enemy.

My testimony is not one of condemnation but of God's ability to rescue, redeem, and restore. As the body of Christ, we must always approach those who are struggling with love, compassion, and prayer. It is through these that the chains of bondage are broken and lives are transformed.

These testimonies serve as compelling evidence that deliverance is possible for those struggling with same-sex attraction. While each journey is unique, a shared thread runs through their stories—a deep sense of emptiness and an unrelenting search for fulfillment. In the end, only God could fill the void within them.

A central theme emerges from each testimony: a transformative encounter with God. As Revelation 12:11 declares, "They triumphed over him by the blood of the Lamb and by the word of their testimony." These individuals found victory through the redeeming power of Jesus and the boldness of their testimony, breaking the enemy's strongholds as they surrendered their lives to God.

Chapter 7: They Have Souls; *What's Behind Their Why?*

The primary purpose of this chapter is to highlight that individuals in the LGBTQ community, like everyone else, have souls that are precious in the eyes of God. While this truth should be self-evident within the Body of Christ, I believe that when it comes to homosexuality, much of the Church's focus tends to be directed more at the sin than at the soul. This misplaced emphasis often blinds believers to the deeper spiritual roots at play, preventing us from extending the love and discipleship these individuals desperately need.

Genesis 2:7 states, "Then the Lord God formed a man from the dust of the ground and breathed into his nostrils the breath of life, and the man became a living being." This truth is foundational. The breath of God the very Spirit of the Lord was breathed into every human being, including those struggling with same-sex attraction. Each soul holds immense value because it carries the essence of God within it.

Sin, regardless of its form, does not separate us from God's love; rather, it separates us from His holiness, purpose, and covenant. The

Church must remain vigilant in remembering that those caught in the bondage of sin are still souls in need of redemption.

But the question remains: Why are so many struggling with these particular sins, and what lies at the root of their "why"?

"The Spiritual Roots Behind the "Why"

A key objective of this chapter is to uncover the spiritual forces and traumatic experiences that often lie beneath the surface of same-sex attraction. When we focus solely on outward behavior and sin, we risk overlooking the deeper issues—the spiritual wounds and strongholds that frequently serve as the root cause. In many cases, the seeds of perversion are planted early in life—during childhood, adolescence, and sometimes even at conception.

As we explore the testimonies shared throughout this book, a common thread emerges: many individuals who struggle with homosexuality have experienced sexual abuse, neglect, or other forms of childhood trauma. Some were searching for love and validation but found themselves in relationships or situations that deviated from God's design. These experiences leave them vulnerable to spiritual forces that exploit pain and deepen bondage. I will further discuss this, along with how generational curses create significant spiritual breaches, leading to unexplainable warfare.

Taking the blinders off

One of the most powerful moments in my walk with God was when the blinders finally came off, and I could truly see what I was up against. For so long, I walked in darkness, making excuses for my behavior, unaware of the spiritual forces influencing my life. I was blind to the warfare happening around me and within me. But when Jesus entered my life and began to transform me, I finally understood the meaning of the scripture: I was blind, but now I see (John 9:25). That moment of clarity is what so many people are missing, and as leaders—as disciples—it is our responsibility to help others remove those blinders too.

Spiritual warfare is real, and it happens whether we acknowledge it or not. The enemy thrives in our ignorance. When we fail to recognize what we are fighting, we end up battling in the dark, swinging aimlessly at things we cannot see. But when the blinders come off—when we truly open our spiritual eyes—we are no longer on an uneven playing field. We begin to recognize the enemy's tactics for what they are. We see the patterns, the strongholds, the generational curses, and the schemes designed to keep us bound. Most importantly, we gain the authority to fight back effectively. We learn what to pray against, what to rebuke, and how to stand firm in the armor of God.

I have been in that dark place lost, broken, and making excuses for my sin because I simply did not know any better. I justified my actions, convincing myself that my struggles defined me, all while the enemy tore my life apart piece by piece. But once God opened my eyes, I saw the truth. I recognized the forces warring against my soul and my purpose. Now, I am committed to helping others experience that same freedom. It is not enough for me to walk in the light I am called to be a light and a voice that helps others see the truth as well.

As leaders, we have a mandate to help people remove their blinders. But before we can do that, we must first remove our own. We must look beyond the surface with holy lenses and the heart of God. It is not just about calling out sin—it is about helping people see the very forces that seek to destroy them: the spirits, the strongholds, the generational curses, and the lies that keep them bound. We must guide them to the truth so they can not only see themselves clearly but also recognize the enemy's strategies for what they are.

Because when they see, they can fight.

When they see, they can break free.

And when they see, they can finally step into the fullness of their God-given purpose.

That is the power of taking the blinders off. And that is the mission the church must be committed to.

Incubus and Succubus Spirits: Sowing Seeds of Perversion

A critical spiritual reality that must be addressed is the influence of incubus and succubus spirits—demonic entities known for planting seeds of sexual immorality and perversion, particularly during sleep. These spirits are often linked to sexual dreams, nightmares, and torment, preying upon individuals when they are most vulnerable. The incubus is a male spirit that preys on women, while the succubus is a female spirit that targets men. However, these entities can also attack individuals of the same sex. They are not merely folklore but ancient spiritual forces that seek to corrupt God's design for sexuality, often taking root as early as adolescence.

While modern society considers the emergence of sexual desires during puberty as "normal" or "natural," we must recognize that the enemy exploits this critical stage of development to plant seeds of lust and confusion. These spirits take advantage of such vulnerability, masquerading as natural desires when, in reality, they are anything but.

Ephesians 6:12 warns us: "For our struggle is not against flesh and blood, but against the rulers, against the authorities, against the powers of this dark world and against the spiritual forces of evil in the heavenly realms." These spirits infiltrate lives through open doors, often using trauma, molestation, and early exposure to pornography as gateways. They subtly introduce ideas and desires that mimic the normal progression of puberty but are, in truth, distortions of God's design.

Many individuals who experience same-sex attraction began struggling with these feelings at an early age. What is often overlooked is that these desires are not always rooted solely in biology or psychology but are also part of a spiritual assault on identity. **Hosea 4:6** states, "My people are destroyed for lack of knowledge." The Church must acknowledge that the enemy has long been waging a spiritual war for souls, starting even before children reach their teenage years.

The Battle for the Mind: Recognizing the Spiritual Strongholds

As the Body of Christ, we must not only address the outward manifestations of sin but also recognize the spiritual forces behind them. It is essential to understand that homosexuality, like other forms of sexual immorality, often stems from deeper spiritual influences and experiences that shape an individual's struggles.

Many who wrestle with this sin have been exposed to perverse spirits, such as incubus and succubus, which sow seeds of confusion, lust, and rebellion. These spirits take advantage of moments of vulnerability whether through abuse, neglect, or the subtle yet pervasive influence of culture and media. Once planted, these seeds take root, growing into a web of confusion and spiritual bondage.

As the Church, our response must not be condemnation but compassion. We must see these individuals not as abominations but as souls engaged in a spiritual battle, in need of guidance, truth, and deliverance.

Generational Curses: The Roots That Bind

Another key factor to consider is the role of generational curses. When I mentioned that spiritual breaches can occur even at conception, this is one of the most significant ways they manifest. While many recognize the impact of sexual abuse, neglect, and emotional trauma as gateways for the enemy to exploit an individual's pain, there is an even deeper root that often goes unaddressed: generational curses and the influence of bloodline sin. These spiritual strongholds can begin their work long before a person is even aware of their identity—even, as I said, at the moment of conception.

Generational curses are spiritual strongholds passed down through family lines, often as a result of unrepented sins, occult practices, or cycles of dysfunction that give the enemy legal access to a bloodline. The Bible references this in Exodus 20:5, where God warns of visiting the iniquities of the fathers upon their children unto the third and fourth generation. These inherited spiritual breaches can manifest in various ways, including struggles with identity, sexual confusion, addiction, and emotional brokenness.

When an individual is conceived within a bloodline still burdened by these curses, the enemy can exploit this spiritual vulnerability, gaining access through the very umbilical cord—the source of life-giving blood and nutrients—allowing demonic influences to attach from the very beginning.

This spiritual breach is one reason why many individuals genuinely believe they were born that way. In a sense, they were—but not because God created them that way. Rather, the enemy capitalized on an unhealed, unrepented generational wound. These attachments often go unnoticed and can lead to deeply ingrained feelings, desires, and attractions that seem innate but are, in reality, spiritual in origin.

Without proper spiritual discernment, counseling may only address surface behaviors rather than the deeply rooted strongholds affecting the soul and spirit.

Breaking generational curses requires more than mere conversation and coping mechanisms—it demands spiritual warfare, deliverance, and the application of the blood of Jesus to cleanse and restore what has been corrupted in the bloodline. True discipleship must acknowledge these deeper spiritual dynamics, guiding individuals toward complete freedom. It is essential to help them understand that while the struggle may feel intrinsic, God provides a way out through healing, deliverance, and the renewal of their minds (Romans 12:2). Only then can they walk in the identity God originally intended for them, free from the chains of generational sin.

A devastating example of this, particularly within the African American community, can be traced back to the practice of buck breaking during the era of slavery.

So, what is buck breaking? According to a user on Urban Dictionary, it is defined as "the rape and sodomization of rebellious African slaves in the southern United States." In essence, buck-breaking was the brutal sexual assault of enslaved African men by white slave owners. No male—young or old—was spared from this horrific practice. Slave masters employed buck-breaking as a form of punishment, humiliation, and psychological domination. The primary goal was to break the spirit of Black male slaves, stripping them of their dignity and authority. By publicly dehumanizing them, slaveholders sought to crush any thoughts of rebellion at a time when uprisings among the enslaved were increasingly common.

Although some have attempted to dismiss buck-breaking as a myth, historical evidence strongly suggests that these atrocities did occur. The consequences of such heinous acts extend far beyond physical abuse; they embedded deep-rooted generational trauma and perversion, creating spiritual breaches that cursed bloodlines for generations on both sides of the atrocity.

When an ancestor experiences such extreme violation, it can open a door to the spirit of perversion, which then travels down through the generations, attaching itself to future descendants. This generational curse continues until someone, through deliverance and the power of God, breaks the cycle. This is the essence of a generational curse a spiritual inheritance that afflicts the lives of descendants who were not even present for the original sin.

Exodus 20:5 The Bible warns that the iniquities of the fathers will be passed down to the third and fourth generations. These curses can manifest in various forms addiction, sexual immorality, or spiritual confusion but they can be broken through the power of the Holy Spirit.

Word Curses

Another powerful form of a curse comes through word curses— negative, destructive words spoken over someone that plant seeds of confusion, pain, and spiritual breaches. In Ricardo's testimony, we see how the repeated comments people made about him—telling him he looked like a girl and calling him a girl throughout his childhood— created a deep spiritual wound. These words, spoken over him time and time again, sowed seeds of confusion and identity struggles, ultimately leading him to believe he was meant to become a woman. This is the dangerous power of spoken words. Proverbs 18:21 reminds us, "Death and life are in the power of the tongue: and they that love it shall eat the fruit thereof." Our words have the power to build up or to destroy, to bless or to curse. When harmful words are spoken repeatedly—especially over children—they can open doors to spiritual oppression just as much as sinful actions can.

This is why we must be extremely careful with the words we speak, particularly to and about our children. Words plant seeds in the spirit, whether they are seeds of life or seeds of destruction. When we carelessly label our sons as "faggots," "punks," or "soft," or call our daughters "dykes" or "tomboys," we are speaking curses into their lives. These labels create spiritual breaches that give the enemy access to manipulate and confuse their identity. James 3:6 warns, "The tongue also is a fire, a world of evil among the parts of the body. It corrupts the whole body, sets the whole course of one's life on fire, and is itself set on fire by hell." The words we speak can either ignite purpose or fuel destruction.

Many children and people in general have been bullied not only by their peers but also by the very words spoken over them by family, friends, and even church members. Instead of mocking or criticizing behaviors especially when young boys display effeminate traits the church must rise up and lead with compassion and wisdom. If a young man behaves effeminately in church, the answer is not ridicule but mentorship. Titus 2:6-7 instructs, "Encourage the young men to be self-controlled. In everything set them an example by doing what is good." Strong, godly men in the church should lead by example, guiding young boys in their identity and teaching them to walk in the authority God has given them. The goal is to bind the spirit of effeminacy, not the child, and to speak life over them.

Likewise, for young women struggling with identity, rather than shaming them, we should affirm who they are in Christ. Spiritually mature women should step in to guide and disciple younger women, helping them grow in faith and character (Titus 2:3-5). Word curses must be broken, and the only way to do that is by replacing destructive words with life-giving truth. Ephesians 4:29 instructs, "Let no corrupting talk come out of your mouths, but only such as is good for building up, as fits the occasion, that it may give grace to those who hear."

As the body of Christ, we must commit to speaking words that edify, uplift, and heal. We are called to help individuals see themselves as God sees them removing harmful labels and replacing them with words that affirm their true, God-given identity. When we break word curses and speak life, we open the door for healing, restoration, and true transformation.

Leviathan and the Spirit of Pride

One of the most powerful strongholds associated with the LGBTQ community is the spirit of Leviathan—a spirit of pride and rebellion. Job 41:34 describes Leviathan as "king over all the children of pride." The widespread celebration of pride in today's society is a clear indication of Leviathan's influence. This spirit not only fosters rebellion against God's design but also leads individuals to embrace sin as an integral part of their identity, making deliverance even more difficult.

Pride becomes a barrier to repentance. As long as individuals are encouraged to "celebrate" their sin, they remain bound by the spirit of Leviathan, believing they have no need for change. The Church's role is to confront this spirit with truth—but to do so in love, offering the freedom that comes through the power of Jesus Christ.

Spiritual Warfare and the Call to Discipleship

The Church must recognize that we are not merely addressing social or psychological issues; we are engaged in spiritual warfare. As **Ephesians 6:12** reminds us, our weapons are not carnal but mighty through God for the pulling down of strongholds. The spirit of homosexuality is a powerful stronghold, one that requires spiritual weapons to break its grip.

If the Body of Christ is to effectively disciple individuals in the LGBTQ community, our focus must not be on human efforts to change people but on leading them to Jesus the One who transforms lives. As we minister to those who struggle, we must be vigilant in recognizing the spiritual forces at work and address the root of the issue through prayer, fasting, and deliverance.

One of the key purposes of this book is to challenge the Body of Christ to re-evaluate its approach to discipling individuals in the LGBTQ community. Homophobia the rejection and condemnation of individuals based on their sexual orientation inflicts deep wounds. It fosters rejection and drives people further away from God's love and healing. However, passivity the outright acceptance of a lifestyle without addressing sin is equally harmful. It denies individuals the truth of God's Word and the freedom that comes from living in alignment with His design.

Both extremes homophobia and passivity constitute spiritual malpractice. Neither approach reflects the true nature of God or His holiness. To effectively disciple those struggling with same-sex attraction, the Church must adopt a balanced approach one that is firm in truth yet rich in love. This balance allows us to walk in the power and authority of God, boldly proclaiming His truth while demonstrating His love in a way that draws people to Christ, the ultimate healer and restorer of souls. leading people toward freedom in Christ.

This balanced approach calls for righteous judgment—not to condemn souls to hell, but to lead them to the One who restores and transforms. The goal of discipleship should never be merely to expose sin but to guide individuals to Christ, the only one who can break strongholds and generational curses.

When we truly understand the spiritual battle at hand, we will disciple with both compassion and conviction, leading people toward freedom in Christ. By recognizing the deep-seated roots behind behaviors and addressing them with love, prayer, and deliverance, we can help bring healing and freedom to those who have been in bondage for generations.

Conclusion

In closing, the Body of Christ must recognize the profound impact of generational curses and spiritual breaches in discipling those struggling with same-sex attraction. By addressing the root causes and leading individuals to Christ with both love and truth, we can break cycles of spiritual oppression and guide them into the freedom and wholeness found only in a relationship with God.

The Church has often fallen short in its discipleship of these individuals, placing excessive focus on outward behavior while neglecting the deeper spiritual roots of the struggle. A more effective approach requires understanding the influence of incubus and succubus spirits, the role of generational curses, and the stronghold of Leviathan. With this knowledge, we can minister with greater wisdom and compassion.

Victory in this battle is not achieved through condemnation or silence but through the wisdom of God and the power of the Holy Spirit.

As the Body of Christ, our calling is not to change people ourselves but to bring them to Jesus the One who breaks every chain. By uprooting the seeds of perversion and confronting the spiritual forces at work, we can lead souls out of bondage and into the true freedom that only Christ can offer.

Chapter 8: We Can't Save Everyone

As disciples of Christ, our hearts are often filled with a deep desire to see every person we encounter transformed by the power of the gospel. We long to witness people set free from the chains of sin, walking in the abundant life that only Jesus can provide. However, while discipleship calls us to share salvation with all, we must also acknowledge a difficult truth not everyone will accept it. Some will hear the gospel and reject it, while others may never feel the conviction or desire to be freed from their bondage. Scripture affirms this reality, and recognizing it allows us to direct our efforts with wisdom.

In our zeal to disciple and spread the gospel, we may sometimes overlook the sobering truth that some hearts are hardened beyond repentance. **Romans 1:28** speaks of those who have been given over to a "reprobate mind" a state in which, after persistently rejecting God, they are abandoned to their sinful desires. In His sovereignty, God allows them to remain in their chosen rebellion. They become desensitized to sin, unresponsive to truth, and beyond the conviction of the Holy Spirit. This is not an easy reality to accept, but it is one that Jesus Himself acknowledged.

When Jesus sent out His disciples, He instructed them not to waste time on those who rejected the message. **In Matthew 10:14**, He said,

"If anyone will not welcome you or listen to your words, leave that home or town and shake the dust off your feet." This serves as a stark reminder that while we are called to spread the gospel, we are not responsible for those who willfully reject it.

There are times when persistently pursuing someone who has no desire to accept Christ is not only fruitless but spiritually draining. It can lead to burnout and hinder your own spiritual growth. That is why discernment is crucial we must recognize when to step back and trust God to work in their hearts in His own way and time.

Matthew 7:6 reinforces this principle: "Do not give what is holy to the dogs; nor cast your pearls before swine, lest they trample them under their feet, and turn and tear you in pieces." This scripture emphasizes the importance of wisely investing our spiritual energy and resources. While the gospel is meant for all, it should not be forced upon those who openly despise it. There is a profound difference between someone struggling with sin and seeking answers, and someone who has fully embraced their sin while remaining hostile to the truth.

This chapter, and indeed this entire book, is not intended for those who have hardened their hearts beyond conviction or who have embraced rebellion against God without remorse. Romans 1:24-25 states that God "gave them up in the lusts of their hearts to impurity" because they exchanged the truth of God for a lie. These individuals have deliberately rejected God's grace, and tragically, some may never turn back. We are not called to chase after those who have chosen to remain in darkness; instead, we are called to focus on those whose hearts remain open to the voice of the Lord.

This book is written for those searching for answers for those who feel the pull of God on their hearts yet find themselves entangled in sin. These individuals may not have fully embraced the truth, but they are not hostile toward it. They wrestle with the conflict between their desires and the conviction of the Holy Spirit. They may feel trapped in cycles of sin, longing for a way out a path to deliverance and transformation. These are the souls we are called to reach, the ones who yearn for freedom but do not yet know how to find it.

Jesus' invitation in **Matthew 11:28** is extended to these weary souls: "Come to me, all you who are weary and burdened, and I will give you rest." This message is for them the burdened, the weary, those who feel the weight of their sin yet struggle to break free. It is for their sake that we labor. Our mission as disciples is to guide them to Christ, the One who can break every chain and set them free. Yet, it is crucial to remember that we are not the saviors; only Jesus can redeem. Our role is to faithfully deliver the message and lead others to the foot of the cross. The work of salvation belongs to God alone.

As difficult as it is, we must accept that free will grants people the choice to follow Christ or remain in their sin. Luke 19:41-44 offers a glimpse into Jesus' sorrow over those who reject Him. As He approached Jerusalem, He wept over the city, lamenting that they had missed the day of their visitation. This serves as a profound reminder that even Jesus perfect in love and truth was rejected by many. Not all will accept the invitation to salvation, and while this reality should grieve us, it must not deter us from our mission.

Some people love their sin and remain content in their rebellion. **John 3:19** states, "Light has come into the world, but people loved darkness instead of light because their deeds were evil." For some, the comfort of their sin is more appealing than the freedom Christ offers. They have no desire for deliverance and will not respond to the gospel message. These are not the individuals we are called to disciple, for they have hardened their hearts and rejected the truth.

However, for those who are searching for those weighed down by guilt, shame, and confusion, longing for a way out we must remain diligent in our efforts. Many of these individuals battle suicidal thoughts, believing there is no hope for them. They may feel consumed by their sin, convinced that the only escape is death. For these souls, we must proclaim a message of hope, pointing them to Jesus as the ultimate answer to their struggles. Their way out is not through despair but through the transformative power of Christ..

2 Corinthians 5:17 reminds us, "Therefore, if anyone is in Christ, the new creation has come: The old has gone, the new is here!" This is the promise we offer to those who seek Him. The burdens and chains of the old life can be left behind, replaced by the freedom found in Christ available to anyone who comes to Him with a repentant heart.

We cannot save everyone, but we are called to reach those searching for the truth those whose hearts are open to the message of the gospel. Our mission is to be faithful in presenting the truth, discipling those willing to receive it, and walking alongside them on their journey to deliverance and transformation. Ephesians 5:11 instructs us: "Have nothing to do with the fruitless deeds of darkness, but rather expose them." While we are called to expose the darkness, only the Holy Spirit can bring true conviction and lead a person to repentance.

We labor for those who are still willing to hear the truth, trusting God to bring the increase. We are called to plant seeds of hope, water them with love and truth, and believe that in His perfect timing, God will bring about transformation.

Chapter 9: Have We Failed Them?

In the journey of faith, many individuals with same-sex attractions find themselves at a crossroads longing for a deeper relationship with the Lord yet struggling to reconcile their experiences with their faith. This raises an important question: Has the Church failed in its call to disciple these individuals and others?

For years, the Church's stance on same-sex attraction has often been characterized by a legalistic approach, compelling those who struggle with such feelings to hide in fear of rejection and condemnation. This unspoken rule created a facade of righteousness while leaving many to wrestle silently with their struggles. Instead of finding refuge in the body of Christ, they were forced into secrecy, fearing exposure and judgment rather than experiencing the freedom Christ promises (Galatians 5:1).

While the intent behind this legalistic approach may have been to uphold doctrinal purity, it often left little room for grace and transformation. As a result, countless individuals felt alienated, trapped in a culture of shame rather than one of healing. Yet, the heart of the gospel is to draw near to the broken (Psalm 34:18), leading them into the redeeming love of Jesus Christ, where chains of sin are broken and lives are transformed.

However, as societal views evolved and a new revolution of pride emerged, many began stepping forward without repentance. This shift exposed the Church's unpreparedness to respond with compassion, prompting a reactionary return to legalism and condemnation rather than understanding and grace. Fearful that extending grace might be perceived as condoning sin, many within the Church focused solely on condemning behavior, overlooking the path to redemption and freedom. Yet, the message of the gospel is never one of condemnation but of restoration (John 3:17).

Authentic relationships are foundational to true discipleship. Jesus modeled this by engaging with individuals on a personal level, understanding their hearts, and demonstrating love despite their struggles (John 4:1-26). He did not shy away from addressing sin, yet He never allowed it to prevent Him from reaching the person behind it. His encounter with the Samaritan woman at the well is a profound example rather than condemning her, He spoke truth with grace, revealing a path toward redemption.

The Church, therefore, must do the same. In a world quick to judge, individuals struggling with same-sex attraction often face condemnation rather than compassion. Yet, as the body of Christ, we are called to emulate Jesus' example building relationships rooted in love, understanding, and truth. True discipleship means walking alongside these individuals, engaging in authentic, life-on-life mentorship that draws them closer to Christ. As Paul wrote in Galatians 6:1, "Brothers and sisters, if someone is caught in a sin, you who live by the Spirit should restore that person gently."

Restoration, not rejection, must be our focus. Our mission is discipleship that heals rather than wounds, offering grace while pointing to the transforming power of Christ. **our primary role is not to change people but to lead them to the One who does the changing—God Himself.** The Word of God makes it clear that transformation is the work of the Holy Spirit, not our own. Our role is to plant seeds of faith, share the truth, and guide others to Jesus, but the deep, inner work of change belongs to God alone.

As Paul writes in 1 **Corinthians 3:6-7:** "I planted the seed, Apollos watered it, but God has been making it grow. So neither the one who plants nor the one who waters is anything, but only God, who makes things grow." This passage reminds us that we often waste valuable time trying to force change in others, focusing on aspects of their lives that are beyond our control. Instead, we are called to do our part plant the seed of God's Word, nurture it with love and prayer, and trust Him to bring the growth.

Our desire is for people to encounter God personally, to experience His love, and to be transformed by it.

When someone **encounters God**, The transformation happens naturally. Once people encounter His glory, His love, and His presence, the grip of sin begins to weaken. Conviction arises not from external pressure by the Church but through the Holy Spirit working within them. Romans 2:4 reminds us that it is God's kindness that leads us to repentance. As individuals deepen their relationship with God and are filled with the Holy Spirit, they become increasingly aware of the weight of conviction on their hearts. **sin begins to fall away**. This is the transformation we long to see the kind only God can bring about.

Our task, as disciples, is to **lead them to this encounter**. We should desire for people to know God not merely through rules and doctrines, but through a personal, transformative relationship with Him. When someone truly encounters God, experiences His love, and allows His Holy Spirit to dwell within them, their life begins to change in ways they never imagined. **convictions naturally follow**. The desire to please God grows within them, and the temptations of the flesh begin to lose their hold. As their love for God deepens, sin becomes less appealing, for their hearts are now set on living for Him.

This is why it is so important for us... (sentence incomplete; please provide the full thought for refinement. to **focus on the right things** Our mission is to introduce people to Christ, teach them the truth of God's Word, and pray for them to be filled with the Holy Spirit. We desire for them to fall deeply in love with the Lord, experiencing His overwhelming love and presence. Rather than relying on human persuasion, we trust the Holy Spirit to convict hearts and transform lives. It is through **relationship** both with us and with God that true discipleship happens.

Commitment to Biblical Truth remains paramount. In a culture that increasingly resists absolute truth, the Church must courageously uphold scriptural teachings. However, this must always be done with grace, recognizing that transformation is God's work (1 Corinthians 6:9-11). We cannot abandon the truth of God's Word in our pursuit of love. It is not loving to distort the Scriptures to make them more palatable, nor is it loving to ignore the real spiritual consequences of sin.

Yet, deliverance and healing take time, and we must be patient, committing ourselves to the process of walking with those we disciple. Transformation is often a gradual process—sanctification, after all, is a lifelong journey (Philippians 1:6). As the Church, we must be equipped with the spiritual wisdom and tools necessary to guide others effectively, combining biblical truth with compassionate support. We must make it clear that transformation is possible through Christ. As Paul reminds us in 2 Corinthians 5:17, "Therefore, if anyone is in Christ, the new creation has come: The old has gone, the new is here!"

So, have we failed discipleship? Perhaps. But it is not too late to recalibrate our efforts. By returning to the foundational principles of love, truth, and genuine relationship with Christ, we can become more effective disciplers, guiding those struggling with same-sex attraction toward the transformative power of a life in Christ. We must reflect, repent, and rebuild our approach to discipleship, focusing on leading individuals toward the redemptive power of Christ rather than simply condemning their actions.

This recalibration requires a shift from surface-level condemnations to deep, intentional discipleship. As society continues to evolve, the Church must respond not with fear or condemnation but with a renewed commitment to Christ-centered discipleship that balances both truth and love. Individuals began stepping out boldly without repentance, challenging the Church's readiness to respond. This shift has revealed our lack of preparedness, pushing us to confront the need for a more balanced, grace-filled approach that still holds fast to biblical principles.

The Church's previous reflexive return to legalism, emphasizing condemnation over compassion, has proven ineffective in addressing the deeper issues faced by individuals grappling with same-sex attraction. This reaction alienates rather than heals. Instead, we must embody Christ's love in our discipleship efforts, offering a pathway to redemption rather than rejection.

Reclaiming Our Call to Discipleship

By confronting these challenges with truth, love, and a commitment to transformation, we can reclaim our calling to disciple all individuals. We must offer a message that points toward the freedom found in Christ and a life of purpose beyond cultural labels and struggles with sin.

The story of Zacchaeus (Luke 19:1-10) reminds us that Jesus saw beyond the sin and into the heart of a man desperately in need of salvation. It was not condemnation that changed Zacchaeus, but the acceptance and truth of Christ's presence in his life.

Our mission is not merely to condemn but to disciple, to love, and to lead others to Christ—the ultimate source of freedom and deliverance.

Let us not falter in our mission but instead rise to the challenge. The journey of discipleship is not easy, but through authentic relationships, a commitment to biblical truth, and the guidance of the Holy Spirit, we can effectively lead others to the transformative power of Christ.

We must be willing to bear the weight of walking alongside those who struggle, trusting that the same God who began a good work in them will be faithful to complete it (Philippians 1:6). Our responsibility is to remain steadfast in the task of discipleship, knowing that the harvest is plentiful, but the laborers are few (Matthew 9:37).

The Church must move beyond its past failings and embrace its role as a community of redemption, healing, and unwavering love.

Chapter 10: Counseling Through the Deliverance Process

One of the major shortcomings of the church in addressing same-sex attraction is the lack of Christian counseling resources. While spiritual deliverance is essential, many individuals struggling with homosexuality also face deep emotional and psychological wounds—wounds that require more than prayer and sermons. Churches must be equipped with counseling resources to help individuals process their struggles in a safe and compassionate environment.

As the testimonies in this book demonstrate, many individuals in the LGBTQ community, myself included, have experienced trauma, abuse, and rejection. These painful experiences often contribute to struggles with same-sex attraction. For instance, Ricardo shared how he was constantly called a girl, leading him to believe he should become one. Words have power, and such verbal abuse can leave deep spiritual and emotional scars.

The church must provide Christian counseling that addresses not only the sin but also the pain and trauma behind it. For too long, the church has either taken a fire-and-brimstone approach, driving people further away, or has been passive and accepting, denying the need for healing and deliverance. Neither approach offers true freedom.

The Word of God instructs us in James 5:16 to "confess your sins to each other and pray for each other so that you may be healed." Healing comes through confession, accountability, and prayer. But how can individuals confess their struggles if they fear judgment, rejection, or misunderstanding? The church must create spaces where people feel safe to share their burdens, knowing they will be met with compassion and biblical wisdom, not condemnation.

A key part of this counseling process is understanding that deliverance is not always immediate. As the testimonies reveal, deliverance from same-sex attraction often involves a journey—one that requires prayer, discipleship, and counseling. While God can perform instant miracles, He often works through a gradual process of healing and transformation. Christian counselors, pastors, and leaders must walk alongside individuals throughout this journey, offering consistent support. If they desire Christ, we must lead them to Him.

It is also important to recognize that mental health and spiritual health are deeply connected. Depression, anxiety, and suicidal thoughts are common among individuals struggling with same-sex attraction, especially those who feel torn between their desires and their faith. The church must be equipped to address these mental health concerns. This does not mean replacing spiritual deliverance with secular therapy but rather integrating biblical counseling with a compassionate understanding of mental health issues.

Additionally, churches must acknowledge that not every pastor or leader is equipped to handle the complexities of same-sex attraction, trauma, or mental health struggles. That is why it is crucial for churches to have trained Christian counselors or to partner with Christian counseling services that can provide the specialized care needed.

Prayer, deliverance, and counseling must work together as essential components of discipleship. Our mission is to lead people to the feet of Christ, where true transformation takes place. However, effective discipleship requires a holistic approach caring for individuals spiritually, emotionally, and physically.

It is also crucial to recognize the role of apologetics in the counseling process. Apologetics is not about winning arguments but about defending our faith with truth and love. 1 Peter 3:15 urges us to always be prepared to give an answer for the hope we have, yet to do so with gentleness and respect. When counseling individuals struggling with same-sex attraction, we must listen to their concerns, acknowledge their pain, and respond with biblical truth anchored in compassion.

In conclusion, the church must rise to the challenge of offering holistic discipleship to those seeking deliverance from same-sex attraction. This includes providing biblical counseling, addressing mental health with wisdom, and equipping ourselves with apologetics to defend the faith while offering hope. Our goal is not merely to lead individuals to a moment of deliverance but to walk with them through their healing

journey, ensuring they experience the full freedom that Christ offers

Chapter 11: Knowing Better to Do Better

Today, it seems that everyone knows someone who identifies as gay or has come out of the closet. Homosexuality has not only become normalized but is also widely celebrated so much so that America dedicated an entire month to recognizing it. That was, of course, before President Trump's executive order rescinded the observance.

To the Body of Christ, this celebration felt outrageous truthfully, it was. Many saw it as a direct affront to God, as the sacred meaning of the rainbow was overshadowed by sin. However, as disciples of Christ, we still have a responsibility to minister to all who are open to receiving the gospel.

I take this research personally because there was a time when I, too, took a legalistic approach to homosexuality. I was deeply homophobic and believed this sin to be the worst of all. I avoided anyone in that community and had no desire to disciple them. I viewed them solely through the lens of their sin rather than as individuals with souls in need of God's grace.

But then, God spoke to my spirit, urging me to look beyond the person and see their heart the way He sees them. That divine encounter transformed my approach to ministry. I came to understand that my role as a disciple was not to condemn but to lead people to the only answer Christ.

The Lord reminded me that the true enemy is not the person but the spiritual forces at work in their lives. The greatest sin isn't homosexuality alone but the bondage, confusion, and perversion that keep people trapped in darkness. God made it clear that I had the answer, and that answer was to be delivered with love. As disciples, we are called to be solutionists. The world is searching for answers, and we carry the truth that has the power to set people free. However, speaking the truth in love is challenging, especially when reaching those who oppose what we stand for. Ministering to the LGBTQ community, in particular, has been difficult because many within it perceive Christians as hateful and judgmental. Unfortunately, the church has at times contributed to that image. To disciple effectively, we must dismantle this narrative standing firm in God's truth while delivering it with love and compassion.

The LGBTQ community often stands in opposition to Christianity, sometimes attempting to defend their lifestyle using scripture. This is why it is crucial for Christians to know God's Word to defend it and to share it with authority, love, and clarity. We must understand that God's truth is unchanging, sharper than any two-edged sword (Hebrews 4:12). The world's attempts to twist or misuse scripture will never stand against the power of divine truth.

However, we must take a moment to understand why the LGBTQ community maintains such a deep connection to Christianity, even when they oppose it. The reason is simple: God has poured out His Spirit on all people (Joel 2:28) and has breathed His life into all of humanity. Whether one realizes it or not, their spirit is naturally drawn to God because He is the source of life. His Spirit calls to the spirit within us, which is why Christianity remains compelling even to those far from God. Yet, this innate attraction to God's truth can be distorted when it is not met with love. This is why we must be equipped to respond to the LGBTQ community with biblical truth while reflecting the love of Christ.

Through research, it has become evident that the most effective way to disciple those struggling with homosexuality is through a balanced approach one that aligns with scripture. We must stand firm in truth while delivering it with love, guiding people toward Jesus rather than pushing them away with harshness or indifference. If the church fails to embrace this approach, we will continue to fall short in this area of discipleship.

Fear often lies at the root of homophobia, silence, and passive acceptance. But as followers of Christ, we cannot afford to be ruled by fear. Second Timothy 1:7 reminds us, "For God has not given us a spirit of fear, but of power and of love and of a sound mind." We are called to walk boldly in the power of the Holy Spirit neither afraid to engage with the LGBTQ community nor hesitant to speak the truth.

Fear drives us to either lash out in judgment or remain silent, but neither response reflects the heart of God.

To truly reach those in the LGBTQ community who are seeking answers, we must have both the courage to stand on God's truth and the compassion to lead them to the foot of the cross. It is only through the power of Christ that yokes are broken and souls are set free. We must always remember that our battle is not against flesh and blood (Ephesians 6:12), but against the spiritual forces that hold people captive.

As disciples, we must move beyond fear, silence, and judgment. When we know better, we must do better. We are called to engage with the LGBTQ community, offering them the truth of God's Word while demonstrating the love of Christ. Our mission is not to condemn but to guide them toward the freedom and transformation that only a relationship with Jesus can bring.

Moving forward, we must take this responsibility seriously. We can no longer stand on the sidelines, nor can we approach this issue with judgment or passivity. Now that we know better, we must do better leading with courage, wisdom, and the power of the Holy Spirit.

Conclusion: A Call to Courageous Discipleship

This book is the result of both a personal encounter with the Lord and a transformative journey in my understanding of discipleship. For many years, I approached the topic of homosexuality within the church through a legalistic lens, believing that sternness and condemnation were the only paths to correction. This mindset was shaped by my own struggles with this stronghold. I now realize that my disdain for the spirit behind it led me to unfairly judge the individuals themselves. I was wrong. In doing so, I missed critical opportunities to reach people I loved with the message of hope and salvation. I had failed them.

It was only when the Lord confronted me and softened my heart that I saw the error in my approach. God did not call me to win arguments or to judge others, but to plant seeds seeds of salvation, hope, and love. This divine encounter ignited a passion within me to dig deeper, study the spiritual dynamics at play, and equip both leaders and disciples who, like me, may have felt unprepared or uncertain when addressing such a sensitive and divisive issue.

We live in an era of confusion, where society claims to be "woke" yet remains spiritually asleep. In this time of heightened self-awareness and evolving ideologies, many have come to believe that their wisdom surpasses God's truth. The rise of relativism and the New Age movement has infiltrated even the church, leading to a widespread compromise of the gospel. Biblical teachings are often diluted by personal opinions, misinterpretations, and cultural trends. As a result, faith becomes less anchored in the Word of God and more influenced by societal shifts.

Against this backdrop, I felt compelled to write this book—not only as a personal reflection but also as a resource for leaders and disciples navigating the complexities of modern discipleship. I recognize the immense pressure many in ministry face when confronting these issues, especially in a world that increasingly rejects biblical truth in favor of secular ideologies. My hope is that this work provides clarity, wisdom, and a framework for addressing the spiritual needs of the LGBTQ community and others who wrestle with identity, sexuality, and faith.

God did not call His church to isolate itself within the walls of tradition, fear, or comfort. We are commanded to go into the highways and byways, reaching those who are lost, confused, and searching for answers. But in doing so, we must be courageous. We must not shrink back from opportunities to plant seeds of hope, even in difficult or uncomfortable situations. Our role as disciples is not to force transformation, but to offer the message of Christ's transformative power. When we plant seeds of hope, it is God who brings the increase. And it is this hope that we are called to defend.

Theologically speaking, hope is central to the Christian faith. As Paul writes in Romans 8:24, "For in this hope we were saved. But hope that is seen is no hope at all. Who hopes for what they already have?" Our hope lies in the promise of transformation through Christ a hope that transcends human wisdom and cultural shifts. It is this hope that gives us the courage to face the challenges of discipleship in a world that increasingly opposes the gospel.

I pray that this book offers not only insight but also encouragement to those who feel the weight of this responsibility. Whether you are a pastor, a leader, or a disciple of Jesus Christ, know that the work you do matters. Every seed planted, every conversation spoken in love, and every moment of truth shared with compassion has the potential to change lives. We are not called to be silent, nor are we called to compromise. Instead, we are called to stand firm in truth while delivering that truth with grace.

In conclusion, this book began as a dissertation, but through prayer, reflection, and study, it has transformed into a heartfelt call to the Body of Christ to grow in knowledge and disciple more effectively. May it serve as a guide, a source of encouragement, and a reminder that God has fully equipped us for this sacred work.

We must not overlook the opportunities He places before us to share His hope with the world. This is the essence of discipleship, and my prayer is that as you move forward, you do so with courage, wisdom, and the love of Christ.

God bless you.

About the Author

Dr. Jennifer B. Allen is the visionary founder of Kingdom Nations Global Network and Lydia's Crown INC., a 501(c)(3) nonprofit organization dedicated to empowering women who have endured traumatic experiences. Through Lydia's Crown, she provides essential resources and coaching to help women transform unhealthy mindsets and journey toward wholeness. Beyond her work in ministry and advocacy, she co-owns Reflection Photography and Publishing LLC, expanding her creative and entrepreneurial impact.

Although raised in the church, Dr. Allen's journey was marked by seasons of rebellion and self-destruction. She struggled with drug and alcohol addiction, leading to multiple stays in mental health facilities and even facing suicide watch. After reaching a breaking point and narrowly avoiding imprisonment, she surrendered her life to God, embracing her calling as a minister of the Gospel of Jesus Christ.

Dr. Allen holds a bachelor's degree in Business, an MBA, and advanced theological degrees, including a doctoral degree in Christian Counseling and a master's degree in Christian Humanities. She earned these credentials from the School of the Great Commission under the guidance of Dr. Crystal Pugh and Dr. Winford Thompson. Spiritually, she is supported by Bishop Anthony Pelt Sr. at Radiant Living

Christian Center, Church of God in Christ and is mentored by Apostle Ron Toliver in Orlando, Florida.

As a bestselling author, Dr. Allen has shared her life story, including her victorious battle against breast cancer, in her Amazon bestseller, Hostage in the Mirror. The book chronicles her profound journey of faith and healing, illustrating how God's guidance led her to a life she once believed was beyond reach. She has also co-authored several other bestsellers alongside influential figures and has independently published a collection of journals designed to support spiritual and personal growth.

Through Dr. Jennifer B. Allen Ministries, her mission is to guide individuals through their personal journeys of healing and transformation. She emphasizes the necessity of a deep, personal relationship with God the Father, Son, and Holy Spirit, encouraging others to experience the abundant life promised in Jeremiah 29:11.

Dr. Allen's diverse background includes proud service in the United States Marine Corps, as well as extensive leadership experience in both business and ministry. She is a devoted wife, a loving and protective mother, a dedicated daughter, and a supportive big sister.

For inquiries or to connect with Dr. Allen, please visit JenniferBAllen.com.

Appendix: References

1. Nelson, Thomas (1995). The Woman's Study Bible. New King James Version.

2. Scott, Jeffrey (May 2010). Case Studies of Selected Churches with Effective Ministry to Male Homosexual Strugglers. Retrieved from: https://digitalcommons.liberty.edu/cgi/viewcontent.cgi?article=1131&context=fac_dis

3. HRC Foundation (N.D.). Stances of Faith on LGBTQ Issues: Christian Church (Disciples of Christ). Retrieved from: https://www.hrc.org/resources/stances-of-faiths-on-lgbt-issues-christian-church-disciples-of-christ

4. Wikipedia (August 27, 2022). Episcopal Church. Retrieved from: https://en.wikipedia.org/wiki/Episcopal_Church_(United_States)

5. Pulaski, A. & Lihn, S. (2004). Biblical Counseling Manual.

6. Shelmon, Alan (April 08, 2017). Can Churches Discipline for the Sin of Homosexuality? Retrieved from: [https://www.str.org/w/can-

churches-discipline-for-the-sin-of-homosexuality-
](https://www.str.org/w/can-churches-discipline-for-the-sin-of-homosexuality-)

7. 700 Club (2021). Delivered From Homosexuality—"I Was Lost But Now I'm Saved!"* Retrieved from: https://www.youtube.com/watch?v=725gfmMBBW4

8. Focus on the Family (2022). Leaving Homosexuality and Finding Forgiveness. Retrieved from: https://www.youtube.com/watch?v=8k9ajsiOaD4

9. Sims, Ricardo (February 20, 2022). God Delivered Me From the Transgender Lifestyle. Retrieved from: https://www.youtube.com/watch?v=loth8YGuqEg

10. Words Way Christian Ministry (June 30, 2022). Delivered From Lesbianism and So Much More. Retrieved from: https://www.youtube.com/watch?v=lID9wfi3nks&t=697s

11. Somto, Isaac (June 17, 2019). Buck Breaking: How African Male Slaves Were Raped. Retrieved from: [https://vocalafrica.com/buck-

breaking-afrcan-male-slaves/](https://vocalafrica.com/buck-breaking-afrcan-male-slaves/)

12. McDowell, J. (No Date). New Evidence That Demands a Verdict. Independent Doctoral Book. School of the Great Commission. (pp. 1-

www.ingramcontent.com/pod-product-compliance
Lightning Source LLC
Chambersburg PA
CBHW070057100426
42740CB00013B/2857